NEV

THE PENALTIES

The Ultimate
WORLD CUP

QUIZ BOOK

PHIL ASCOUGH

First published 2014

The History Press
The Mill, Brimscombe Port
Stroud, Gloucestershire, GL5 2QG
www.thehistorypress.co.uk

British Library Cataloguing in Publication Data.
A catalogue record for this book is available from the British Library.

ISBN 978 0 7509 5842 4

Typesetting and origination by The History Press
Printed in Great Britain

Contents

Foreword
by Kevin Kilbane

As a young boy growing up in Preston, football was my life.
Like so many other kids worldwide I would play whenever or
wherever I could, whatever the weather. It would sometimes
mean scaling fences with my older brother, looking for
somewhere to play without interference.

One of the few things that could interrupt our pursuit of
becoming the next Ian Rush or Kevin Sheedy was the next
best thing to playing football – watching football.

We always had *Match Of The Day*, but there were relatively
few live games on TV during the 1980s. The only time we saw
foreign footballers was if a British club made it to a final in one
of the European competitions.

That's why Mexico 86 will always feel like the perfect time
in my childhood. We had Michael Laudrup, Michel Platini and
Zico, Josimar, Hugo Sanchez and the incredible Diego Maradona.
These were names I'd heard little or nothing about at that time,
yet there they were – the best players in the world on the TV
almost every day for a month.

I was gutted to have to wait another four years for the
next tournament, but when Italia 90 came round it was even
better because Ireland had qualified under Jack Charlton.

Although I grew up in Lancashire, England, my dream was always to play for Ireland, the birthplace of my mum and dad.

Ireland had a tough group with England, Holland and Egypt but managed to qualify to play Romania – with the brilliant Gheorghe Hagi – in the last 16. Watching Packie Bonner saving the penultimate spot kick in the shoot-out to help Ireland reach the quarter-final was the big high for me during that tournament.

Ireland qualified for USA 94 and although I was on the verge of the first team with Preston North End I didn't really believe I'd ever get the chance to represent my country in a World Cup. But my dream came true and I was fortunate to play every minute for Ireland during Japan and South Korea in 2002.

I'll cherish the memories of that month, the highlight of my playing career. We played Cameroon, Germany and Saudi Arabia and then met Spain in South Korea for a place in the last eight. We went out on penalties, with me feeling heartbroken after my shot was saved. I felt we should have beaten Spain, but that's football. My best and worst memories are about penalty shoot-outs, and while I've never been big on swapping shirts I have Carles Puyol's as a World Cup souvenir.

Most of my time now is spent watching and trying to analyse football in a different way, for viewers and listeners on BBC TV and radio.

I felt incredibly privileged to be invited to join their commentary team for the World Cup in Brazil, covering an occasion which has made a huge impact on my life and given me so many great memories, experiencing a different type of pressure and able to relate to what the players on the pitch are going through. My views aren't always shared by supporters up and down the country but I try to give an unbiased opinion. Again, that's football.

I've worked closely with The Down's Syndrome Association since my 9-year-old daughter Elsie was diagnosed with Down's syndrome at birth. They help so many families like mine by providing help and support during what can be daunting times through various stages of life, and I am proud to help them.

I ran the London Marathon in 2013 and raised around £9,000. It was hard work but worth it. I am continuing my support with all the proceeds from my autobiography going to the Down's Syndrome Association.

Kevin Kilbane began his career with Preston North End and moved to West Bromwich Albion before making more than 300 Premier League appearances for Sunderland, Everton, Wigan Athletic and Hull City. He is Ireland's third most-capped player with 110 appearances, a total that includes all four matches at the 2002 World Cup finals. Kevin is now making his mark as a journalist and broadcaster, notably with the BBC. *Killa: The Autobiography of Kevin Kilbane* is published by Aurum Press and is available in bookshops and online. For more information about football for people with Down's syndrome please visit www.dsactive.org

Assists

Beyond acknowledging the inspiration drawn as a young sports writer years ago from the late Ian Wooldridge, I don't often find the need to thank the *Daily Mail* for anything. But apparently it was Colin Young, their reporter in the north east and a former colleague at the *Hull Daily Mail*, who was first to reach Kevin Kilbane with my request to contribute to this book.

Many thanks Colin; that's a pint I owe you. Thanks also to Ash Lord and his colleagues at Hull City AFC who paved the way, to 'City Till We Die' stalwart Kate Ogram for helpful information about Down's syndrome football activities, and to Niall Quinn for his interest.

Thanks most of all though to Kevin, whose help I sought because of the dignity and respect that became his trademark during a career at the top of the domestic and international game, and which he has since taken into the media as a newspaper columnist, national broadcaster and in his acclaimed autobiography. *Killa: The Autobiography of Kevin Kilbane*, published by Aurum Press, is highly recommended for its honesty and insight, and for Kevin's decision to donate the royalties to the Down's Syndrome Association.

It's not difficult to find information about the World Cup in print or online. The challenge is to sift it, check it, identify the material that can be shaped into questions that will challenge and tease and which will appeal both to casual fans and expert witnesses.

The themes and the questions are all mine, as are any errors and subsequent apologies, and the inspiration is drawn from a small number of reputable sources.

Once again I am grateful to Trevor Bugg and his colleagues at www.11v11.com who work tirelessly to make sure their database on countless football competitions is as accurate and up to date as it can be.

In print, most World Cup compilations of recent years owe something to *The Story of the World Cup* (Faber and Faber), written by Brian Glanville, first published in 1973 and updated on many occasions since then. It is a compelling read and one in which Glanville uses his presence at the heart of the World Cup cauldron to paint some vivid pictures for his readers.

World Cup '66 (Eyre and Spottiswoode) was found hidden away in an antiques gallery in Hull. Edited by Hugh McIlvanney and featuring contributions from John Arlott, Bob Ferrier, Arthur Hopcraft and Tony Pawson it is a collection of the most incisive prose from England's finest football hour. I am grateful to Geoffrey Rhodes for allowing me to borrow the copy that he was given as a boy in October 1966.

Introduction

There I was, sitting in Waterstones, signing copies of *Never Mind the Tigers* when I glanced up to see Niall Quinn – tall, angular, instantly recognisable – fretting about Sunderland and about his homework as a co-commentator later that day for Hull City against Stoke City.

Sensing an opportunity to top-up his Hull City knowledge, he bought one of my books. Seizing the moment, I asked if he could help. I explained that I needed someone to write the foreword for a World Cup quiz book. Ideally someone who had played in the finals, who was respected as a player and who had made his mark in the media. Could he put me in touch with Kevin Kilbane?

Was his look one of disappointment or disbelief as I handed him my business card? Only later did it sink in that the episode was akin to chatting to a pretty girl in the playground only to ask if her friend would go out with me.

The word 'flounce' was invented for such a situation but Quinn, ever the gentleman, said he would see what he could do and strode off towards the TSB, clutching his copy of *Never Mind the Tigers*.

I reckon he probably read the book twice as he mined for inspiration later that day during a match which resembled one of those dull opening group games at the World Cup. I also reckon he'll find this one rather more appealing.

The subject matter helps of course, because only the World Cup can quell the busiest communities into ghost towns, igniting them a couple of hours later into a frenzy of flags and firecrackers, klaxons and car horns.

Never Mind the Penalties will test the credentials of any self-styled World Cup aficionado and bring back memories of the brilliant and bizarre episodes that make the tournament the biggest and best single sporting event on the planet. For novices, the uninitiated, fair-weather fans of big events, it is the ultimate, unofficial bluffers' guide, and might even enable you to finish the sentences started by John Motson.

It's not all about the big teams and nor is it a pat on the back or a slap in the face for the efforts of our own nations. The prominence of some nations over others generally reflects their greater involvement in a tournament which dates back more than 80 years. The frequent references to the English domestic game indicate the extent to which it has evolved, for better or worse, as a result of investment in players from overseas.

When it comes to the heroism and heartbreak of the World Cup, Kevin Kilbane has been there, done it and worn the shirt. Anyone who saw him analysing the festive fixtures on *Match Of The Day 2* in December 2013 will know that Kevin is not the most enthusiastic shirt-swapper but, as his foreword reveals, in Korea 2002 he traded up!

Phil Ascough, 2014

Round

1

1966

We start with 1966 because if England hadn't hosted – and then won – the tournament it's unlikely the World Cup would matter nearly as much as it does. Whether you delight in or deride England's success, this was a remarkable festival, the fall-out from which did much to shape the game in the UK, Ireland and even around the world.

1   At which ground did North Korea play all of their group games at the 1966 finals?

2   Which legendary player scored twice for West Germany in his first World Cup finals appearance, against Switzerland at Hillsborough in 1966?

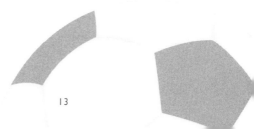

3   Which opponents were branded 'animals' by England
    manager Alf Ramsey, who ordered his players not to
    swap shirts?

4   Defending champions Brazil exited the 1966 tournament
    at the group stage after recording only one win.
    Which team did they beat?

5   What sort of creature was World Cup Willie,
    the official mascot of the 1966 World Cup?

6   Which player scored the only goal of the game in the
    shock of the tournament, North Korea's win over Italy?

7   England only conceded one goal en route to the 1966
    World Cup final. Which player scored it?

8   Which team had two players sent off by the referee in
    their quarter-final match?

9 Which team were the tournament's top scorers, with 17 goals?

10 Which team won the play-off for third place?

11 Which broadcaster secured his place in World Cup history when he remarked: 'Some people are on the pitch ... they think it's all over ... it is now!'

England

England is alphabetically the first of the Home Nations, chronologically the first to compete in the World Cup finals and numerically top of the list for tournaments contested. With so much football going on it's bizarre to look at some of the stories that have made the headlines.

1 Who was the first England player to be selected in the squad for four World Cup finals?

2 Who, in 1967, became the first team to beat England after their World Cup triumph?

3 England didn't make it to the 1974 World Cup, but which future manager played three games in the tournament for his country?

4   Which star of the 1953 FA Cup final had scored England's first goal in the World Cup finals against Chile three years earlier?

5   Who played in three of England's matches in the 1958 finals and years later managed the team in two tournaments?

6   Which player scored England's goal against Germany in 2010 before Frank Lampard's effort was ruled not to have crossed the line?

7   Who was the only England player to score from the spot when they lost a penalty shoot-out to Portugal at the 2006 tournament?

8   Which member of England's World Cup-winning side from 1966 also played first-class cricket for Essex?

9   What was the name of the faith healer who influenced
     Glenn Hoddle during his spell as England coach?

10 Graham Taylor was portrayed as which vegetable by a
     national tabloid newspaper when he resigned as England
     manager after failing to lead the team to the 1994 finals?

11 Which bones in the foot made headline news when
     breaks threatened the presence of David Beckham at
     the finals in 2002, ruled Gary Neville out of the same
     tournament and hampered Wayne Rooney in 2006?

Round

3

Northern Ireland

It's unfortunate that the 1958 Northern Ireland side, which was arguably the finest to reach the World Cup finals, did so before the age of mass media and live television. More recently their expectations have reflected the reality of their resources, but in 1982 they were one of the most exciting teams in the tournament.

1   Who became the youngest player to appear in the World Cup finals when he made his Northern Ireland debut against Yugoslavia in the 1982 World Cup?

2   Who played in Northern Ireland's team at the 1958 World Cup finals and managed the side in the 1982 and 1986 tournaments?

3 Why did the Irish Football Association receive protests from some quarters after Northern Ireland qualified for the 1958 finals?

4 Who scored for Northern Ireland at Windsor Park in September 2005 to inflict England's only defeat of the 2006 World Cup qualifying campaign?

5 Who held the record for the oldest player to appear at the finals when he played his last match in Northern Ireland's 3–0 defeat against Brazil in the 1986 tournament?

6 Which player finished the 1958 finals as one of the top five scorers after netting five goals as Northern Ireland progressed to the quarter-finals?

7 Which player joined Real Mallorca in 1983 and was abused by fans for the goal that earned Northern Ireland victory over the Spanish hosts in the previous year's World Cup?

8   Which opponents scored four times to end Northern Ireland's World Cup hopes in the 1982 finals just as they had in 1958?

9   Which player, whose clubs included Portsmouth, Queens Park Rangers and Southampton, scored Northern Ireland's last goal in the World Cup finals, against Spain, in 1986?

10 Who scored for Northern Ireland when they shocked eventual group winners Russia by winning 1–0 at Windsor Park in the race to qualify for the 2014 World Cup?

11 Which Northern Ireland player was selected with the likes of Pelé and Garrincha for the team of the 1958 World Cup in a poll of journalists who covered the tournament?

Round
4

Republic of Ireland

Strictly speaking not a Home Nation, but impossible to omit given the strength of their links to the rest and the stunning impact on the World Cup of players well known for their performances in the English and Scottish leagues and of fans who bring any tournament to life.

1   Who were Ireland's first opponents in the World Cup finals at Italia 90?

2   After Pat Bonner saved the Romanian Daniel Timofti's penalty, who scored the decisive kick to send Ireland into the 1990 World Cup quarter-finals without having won a match?

3 What was unique about Ireland's group in the first round of the 1994 World Cup?

4 Why did coach Jack Charlton and striker John Aldridge end up in trouble with officials at the 1994 World Cup?

5 Which future Premier League striker scored to set up victory for the Netherlands against Ireland in the 1994 World Cup second round?

6 Which achievement was shared by Robbie Keane of Ireland and Ronaldo of Brazil in the 2002 World Cup finals?

7 Which former captain of the Ireland side succeeded Jack Charlton as manager and led the team to the 2002 World Cup?

8 Goals from Ian Harte and Robbie Keane were enough to earn Ireland victory over which team from the Middle East in a play-off prior to the 2002 finals?

9 Which player scored the crucial equaliser in the group game against the Netherlands that sent Ireland through to the knockout stage in 1990?

10 Ireland missed out on qualification for the 2010 World Cup finals after a handball by which French striker set up the winning goal in a play-off match?

11 Which player, who made more than 300 appearances for Everton, scored Ireland's first goal in the World Cup finals in June 1990?

Round

5

Scotland

Scorers of one of the finest goals in the history of the World Cup finals which delivered one of the competition's greatest upsets, but not quite big enough. Said to be as good as England when England won the trophy, led against Brazil with a Brazilian-style goal in 1982, backed by fans with a unique passion who, in 1978, were said to be planning to travel to Argentina by submarine; something which has never completely been dismissed as merely media spin!

1 Which combative midfielder scored twice as Scotland inflicted the only defeat on the Netherlands on their way to the 1978 World Cup final?

2 Goals from Davie Cooper and Frank McAvennie earned Scotland victory in a play-off for 1986 World Cup qualification against which nation?

3 Which two future managers of Scotland lined up in the side that played two matches at the 1954 World Cup?

4 Which manager, who went on to enjoy huge success at club level, led Scotland during the 1986 World Cup?

5 With qualification for the knockout stages in sight, which team stunned the Scots by pulling off a 3–0 win in Saint-Étienne in 1998?

6 What prompted Scotland fans in October 1996 to sing 'There's only one team in Tallin'?

7 Which opponents made it a hat-trick of heartbreaks when they followed Brazil from 1974 and the Netherlands from 1978 to beat Scotland into the knockout stages on goal difference in 1982?

8 How did Scotland's first manager, Andy Beattie, react to only being allowed by the Scottish FA to take a squad of 13 to the 1954 finals?

9 What World Cup 'first' was achieved by Scotland at the 1974 finals?

10 Which overseas manager – a World Cup winner as a player – resigned from the job of Scotland coach after a poor start to the 2006 qualifying campaign?

11 With two goals in 1974 and one each in 1978 and 1982, which player is Scotland's leading scorer at the World Cup finals?

Round 6

Wales

The section on *Absent Friends* could almost comprise solely players from Wales. At any tournament since the 1960s it's likely that a carefully selected Welshman would have improved any of the participants. Envious glances were cast at John Charles in 1958 and his injury absence from the quarter-finals remains one of football's great 'what-ifs'.

1   Arsenal and Wales keeper Jack Kelsey, ever-present for his country at the 1958 finals, reportedly rubbed what into his hands to help him grip the ball?

2   Wales sealed qualification for the 1958 finals with a play-off win over Israel at which venue?

3   Which player scored Wales' first goal in the World Cup finals, with the equaliser in their opening game against Hungary in the 1958 tournament?

4 Which future superstar announced his arrival on
   the world stage at the age of 17 with the goal
   that eliminated Wales in the quarter-finals of the
   1958 tournament?

5 Wales did the double with home and away wins over
   which opponent during their unsuccessful qualifying
   campaign for the 2014 World Cup?

6 At which venue did Wales lose a crucial World Cup
   qualifier to Scotland in controversial fashion in
   October 1977?

7 Which legends of Welsh football were on the score
   sheet to secure a 2–0 win over Belgium in a World Cup
   qualifier in March 1993?

8 A disastrous 1998 qualifying campaign saw Wales
   record only two wins, both against which minnows of
   European football?

9 John Charles starred at the 1958 World Cup for Wales
   having completed his first season with which Italian club?

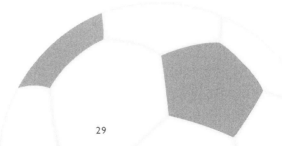

10 A dropped point against which nation at Vetch Field
    in October 1981 led to Wales missing out by goal
    difference on qualification for the 1982 tournament?

11 Which player finished as leading scorer for Wales at the
    1958 World Cup with two goals?

Round

7

Brazil

The most successful nation in the history of the World Cup have lifted the trophy more times than they've been knocked out in the first round. Brazil are synonymous with the World Cup for the number of triumphs and also for the quality of the performances and the ball-on-a-string skills of so many of the players. But in the ten tournaments that followed their 1970 display of brilliance they didn't win any more trophies than Germany, Argentina or Italy.

1   Which team, who inflicted Brazil's first defeat at the 1966 World Cup, had also been the last team to beat them in the tournament, at the quarter-final stage in 1954?

2   Against which opponents did Brazil deliver the first goalless draw in the finals in 1958?

3   At which ground did Brazil play all their matches at the 1966 World Cup, winning only one as they were eliminated in the group stage?

4 What record was achieved by Brazil's flying winger Jairzinho during the 1970 tournament?

5 Who were the opponents in the 1978 finals when referee Clive Thomas controversially blew his whistle for full time as the ball was flying towards the net for what would have been Brazil's winning goal?

6 Which star of the Brazil World Cup teams of 1982 and 1986 spent a month as player-coach of Garforth Town in England's Northern Counties East League in 2004?

7 The same team ended Brazil's World Cup hopes in the 1998 and the 2006 tournaments. Who were they?

8 Which record-breaking striker scored his last World Cup goal for Brazil in the 3–0 win over Ghana at the 2006 tournament?

9   Which team did Brazil play twice – in the group stage and the semi-final – on their way to winning the World Cup for the fifth time in 2002?

10 Who made history by winning the World Cup as a player with Brazil in 1958 and 1962 and again as the team's manager in 1970?

11 Which Brazil player became the youngest to score in a World Cup final when he struck against Sweden in 1958?

Winners

It takes a rare talent and a fortunate combination of circumstances to win the World Cup. Home advantage helped England in 1966, West Germany in 1974, Argentina in 1978 and France in 1998. But in 1982 it hindered Spain who, in South Africa in 2010, won their first title in a competition where the hosts posed no threat. Brazil did the same in the United States and Asia. West Germany won an unsatisfactory final in Italy in 1990; Italy did the same in Germany in 2006. Genius was at the heart of Brazil's triumph in 1970 and Argentina's in 1986, but so was the exhausting heat of Mexico.

1   Uruguay, the winners of the first World Cup tournament, refused to travel to Italy to defend their title in 1934. Why?

2   Which team was the first to win the World Cup away from home?

3 Which team inflicted the only defeat on West Germany during the 1974 World Cup?

4 Which good-luck ritual became a feature of France's successful World Cup campaign in 1998?

5 In 2010, Spain recorded a new low of goals scored by the World Champions with eight during the entire tournament. Which player scored five of them?

6 England's World Cup-winning manager Alf Ramsey had previously coached which team to the English League Championship?

7 Mario Kempes fired Argentina to the 1978 World Cup with six goals. With which Spanish team did he play his league football at the time?

8 Who was the only player to score against Brazil during the knockout stages of their triumphant campaign in 2002?

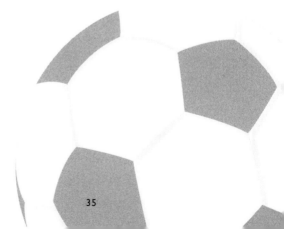

9 Italy have finished as runners-up in the World Cup twice, beaten on each occasion by which team?

10 What was the occasion when Brazil and Germany met for the first time in the World Cup finals?

11 Who is the only player to have won the World Cup three times?

Venues

The selection of venues for the World Cup has become a contest as competitive as the tournament itself. It is also more open, but only in the sense that the needs of players and fans are not always high on the list of criteria. Yet by the time a tournament comes around, any murky dealings are generally forgotten amid the excitement and the ecstasy, the passion and the … erm … plastic horns?

1 What was significant about the match between the United States and Switzerland in Pontiac during the 1994 tournament?

2 The choice of which country as hosts for 2022 prompted debate about moving the tournament from summer to winter because of concerns over soaring temperatures?

3 What was the name of the plastic horn that was popular with fans and provided a degree of wind assistance to the South African team when they hosted the 2010 finals?

4 Which World Cup record was set when Italy met Sweden at Toluca, Mexico, in the 1970 tournament?

5 Why was the match between Uruguay and France at the 1966 tournament played at White City when all the other games in the group took place at Wembley?

6 Which nation was originally selected to host the 1986 finals but missed out because it lacked the facilities to cope with an ever-expanding tournament?

7 Who were the first hosts of a World Cup to be eliminated in the first round of the tournament?

8 Joint hosts were selected for the first time for the 2002 World Cup. Which nations shared the honour?

9 In the voting to decide the hosts for the 1966 World Cup, which country finished second behind England?

10 All the matches in the inaugural 1930 World Cup took place in which city in Uruguay?

11 Which country has submitted the most bids to host the World Cup finals?

Round

10

Upsets

Expanded tournaments increase their capacity to produce shocks. Yes, there were upsets within the 16-team format but there have been more as the numbers have increased to 24 and 32. For the neutral, which, wagers aside, is what the majority of us are for most of the matches, there is no greater World Cup thrill than watching the best in the world being bitten by the underdog. Such matches are our World Cup final, and are often more exciting than the big occasion itself.

1   How did Larry Gaetjens become a part of World Cup history in 1950?

2   Which top side did North Korea famously beat to qualify for the quarter-finals of the 1966 World Cup?

3   Which midfielder scored the only goal as Ireland beat Italy in their opening group game at the 1994 World Cup?

4   Which team playing in only their second World Cup finals
    shocked Italy at the 2010 tournament by securing a
    1–1 draw which helped to send the holders out at the
    group stage?

5   Belgium reached the knock-out stages of the 1994
    World Cup but as one of the best third-placed teams
    after a shock defeat against which minnows in the
    group matches?

6   West Germany thrashed Mexico 6–0 in Argentina in
    1978 but were then held to a goalless draw by which
    World Cup debutants from Africa?

7   The 1990 World Cup opened with a shock as holders
    Argentina went down 1–0 to Cameroon. Which player
    scored the only goal?

8   Which African team finished top of their group and helped
    to take England through with them by producing a
    shock win over Portugal in 1986?

9 Victory for Scotland over the Netherlands in 1978 came too late to bring a place in the knock-out stages as a result of failure to beat which Middle East nation?

10 Holders France were dumped out of the 2002 World Cup at the group stage. They began with defeat against Senegal after Papa Boupa Diop scored the only goal. Which English Premier League club did he join in 2004?

11 As hosts in 1950 Brazil hit seven goals against Sweden and six against Spain before crashing to a shock defeat that handed the World Cup to which team?

Round

II

Controversies

Sex and drugs and forward rolls? There's been all this and more as the World Cup has lurched from one scandal to another. On the field, the minority of players skilled and determined in the art of simulation take encouragement from the appointment of inexperienced match officials. Off-field, particularly at times of assassination and a 'football war', it is more a case of the game being in the wrong place at the wrong time.

1 The murder of Andrés Escobar in 1994 was linked by some investigators to which incident involving the Colombian player at that year's World Cup?

2 Which two nations went to war after a play-off match in 1969 for the following year's World Cup finals ignited underlying political tensions between the two?

3   Which player walked out of Ireland's training camp ahead of the 2002 World Cup after a row about preparations and facilities?

4   Which French player was carried off the pitch after a controversial challenge by West Germany goalkeeper Harald Schumacher in a semi-final at the 1982 World Cup?

5   What was the nationality of the linesman who advised the referee in the 1966 World Cup final that the ball did cross the goal-line from Geoff Hurst's shot for England's third goal?

6   Portugal's 2006 victory over the Netherlands featured four red cards, sixteen yellow cards and one goal. Who scored it?

7   Which Scotland player was sent home from the 1978 World Cup after failing a drugs test as a result of his medication for hay fever?

8 Which team was eliminated from the 1982 World Cup after West Germany and Austria contrived to produce a 1–0 win for Germany, which enabled them both to advance from the group stage?

9 Which country was denied the chance to host the 2006 World Cup after Charles Dempsey ignored his voting instructions from the Oceania Football Confederation?

10 Which woman was at the centre of the row between Wayne Bridge and John Terry, which resulted in Bridge quitting the England squad and Terry being sacked as captain ahead of the 2010 World Cup finals?

11 Which player was headbutted by Zinedine Zidane in the 2006 World Cup final?

Round 12

Howlers

Losing the World Cup before you've even won it takes a special ineptitude, but it's the blunders on the pitch – not all of which are featured here because we can't dwell too much on England – that linger in the memory ... along with some dreadful songs.

1   What was the name of the dog that found the World Cup after it was stolen from an exhibition of stamps in London in 1966?

2   Which essential equipment was missing as Jack Taylor prepared to whistle for the start of the 1974 World Cup final, forcing the English referee to delay the kick-off for a few minutes?

3   Which referee mistakenly showed a yellow card to Josip Šimunić three times during the 2006 match between Croatia and Australia?

4 Why was the Zaire defender Mwepu Ilunga booked during his team's 1974 group game against Brazil?

5 Who caught David Seaman napping with a 40-yard free kick that sailed over the England goalkeeper's head and into the net to give Brazil a 2–1 win in the quarter-finals in 2002?

6 Which Premier League star was expelled from France's 2010 World Cup squad, prompting a bizarre strike by angry teammates?

7 What was the name of the song by Fat Les which became England's unofficial fan anthem of the 1998 World Cup?

8 A blunder by match officials literally handed Diego Maradona and Argentina the lead in the 1986 quarter-final, but which player scored for England in the 2–1 defeat?

9 Rumours ranging from cardiac problems to sponsor interference were rife after which player was picked for the 1998 World Cup final when clearly unfit?

10 Which Brazil player was fined but avoided suspension after faking injury in an incident which brought the dismissal of Turkey's Hakan Ünsal during a group game in 2002?

11 Fans of which nation at the 2010 World Cup were reportedly ordered to remove their shorts because they carried the branding of a competitor to the official tournament beer?

Round

13

No Easy Games?

It's all about preparation and doing your homework, minimising the likelihood of surprises. If you know a bit about World Cup history, including some of the finer details around the big events and the A–Z of such World Cup essentials, such as music and mascots, then you can start rehearsing your goal celebration.

1 Which team, in 1982, beat Argentina with the first goal in an opening game at the finals since 1962?

2 In 1966, Antonio Carbajal became the first player to appear in the finals of five World Cups, but where is he from?

3 Stars of the 1966 World Cup, North Korea were disqualified from the 1970 tournament after refusing to play which team in qualifying?

4   The FIFA Anthem, composed by Franz Lambert, was first played at which tournament?

5   Zakumi, the official mascot for the 2010 World Cup, was based on which creature?

6   Which team was banned from using skin-tight, sleeveless shirts at the 2002 World Cup?

7   Which item of clothing, not normally considered part of a referee's attire, was worn by Jean Langenus when he officiated in the 1930 World Cup final?

8   Which Chilean striker who played for Barnsley and Newcastle United lined up for his own country when England played their first World Cup match in 1950?

9   Which player scored to help West Germany win their quarter-final matches against Northern Ireland in 1958 and England in 1970?

10 Australia made their World Cup finals debut in 1974, but against which nation?

11 Which team at the 1978 tournament became the first from Africa to win a match at the finals?

Round

14

Open Goals

A random selection of questions which really are as menacing as the El Salvadors and North Koreas (2010 vintage) of the World Cup. Any you don't know should be easy to work out. Or guess. If not, it could be the László Kiss of death to your World Cup credibility.

1 In population terms, which is the smallest nation to have won the World Cup?

2 Which national team is known as 'Bafana Bafana'?

3 The World Cup trophy was named after which French lawyer in time for the 1950 tournament?

4 Which England manager quit the job when qualification for the 1978 tournament became unlikely and accepted a coaching role in the United Arab Emirates?

5 All four Home Nations entered the 1950 World Cup with two places up for grabs, but which one indignantly refused to compete in the finals after only finishing second in the qualifying competition?

6 Which is the only nation to have competed in every World Cup finals?

7 All four Home Nations qualified for the finals for the only time in which year?

8 Arthur Ellis, an official at the World Cup finals in 1950, 1954 and 1958, took up a new appointment as the referee in which TV game show, launched in 1966?

9 'Jabulani' attracted criticism from a number of players and coaches during the 2010 tournament, but what was it?

10 Who was the first manager to fail to qualify for the World Cup finals with England?

11 What did László Kiss do in just 8 minutes during the 1982 finals?

Round 15

Marksmen

Goals win games and there have been some sensational scoring feats since Lucien Laurent of France first rippled the net in 1930. In many cases the top scorers are the players from the big teams who reap the rewards of multiple appearances at the finals, but others make an impact in just one tournament – or even one match.

1   Geoff Hurst hit the goals which brought victory for England in the 1966 World Cup final, but which injured striker did he replace after the third game of the tournament?

2   Which striker responded to allegations of diving by plunging headlong across the turf as part of his goal celebrations after joining Tottenham Hotspur in 1994?

3   Which player who had been written off by his country's media responded by finishing as top scorer at the 1982 World Cup with six goals?

4   Which player scored three times at the 2006 tournament to claim a record of 15 World Cup goals and might have had more but for a mysteriously lethargic performance in the 1998 final?

5   Which player single-handedly dragged Portugal back into their 1966 World Cup quarter-final against North Korea by scoring four goals as his team trailed 3–0?

6   Which Poland winger and scourge of England during the qualifying campaign finished the 1974 World Cup as top scorer?

7   Which player set the record for the most goals in a single World Cup tournament, with 13 for France in 1958?

8   Which marksman scored in six of Croatia's seven games at the 1998 tournament, finishing as top scorer and taking his team to third place?

9   Teófilo Cubillas scored a total of ten goals in two tournaments – including two against Scotland in 1978 – for which nation?

10 Which player set a record for most goals in one World Cup match with five, as Russia beat Cameroon 6–1 in 1994 but still failed to reach the knockout stage?

11 Which player's winning goal against Nigeria in the 2002 tournament gave him a total of ten and established him as Argentina's top scorer in the World Cup finals?

Keepers

A drop in the average number of goals per World Cup finals match from between four and five in the 1930s and 1950s to well below three in every tournament since 1962 is evidence of well-organised defences – and better goalkeepers. The most spectacular saves will never be forgotten, and the advent of penalty shoot-outs has turned keepers into potential match-winners, but there are still one or two who might be more at home in the *Howlers* round.

1 FIFA's award for the best goalkeeper in each World Cup was named after which Russian custodian who made his last tournament appearance in 1966, travelling to Mexico only as back-up four years later?

2 And which keeper was the first to win the award after it was introduced for the 1994 tournament?

3 Which player was already celebrating a goal as his powerful header flew towards the bottom corner of the goal only to then be denied by a wonder save from Gordon Banks when Brazil played England in 1970?

4 Which Poland keeper blocked England's route to the 1974 tournament with a world-class display in the final qualifying match at Wembley after being branded a clown by Brian Clough?

5 Which keeper was selected for four consecutive Italian World Cup squads and finally captained his country to glory in 1982 at the age of 40?

6 Who was in goal for Argentina as they triumphed in penalty shoot-outs against Yugoslavia and then Italy but could do nothing with the spot-kick with which Andreas Brehme won the final for West Germany in 1990?

7 Which goalkeeper, known as a penalty and free-kick specialist, scored four goals for Paraguay in their qualifying campaign for the 2002 finals?

8 Who became the first goalkeeper to win two World Cup finals, taking his place in the Brazil teams of 1958 and 1962?

9 Against which team in 2006 did Portugal's Ricardo set a record for the most saves in a penalty shoot-out, with three?

10 Which eccentric keeper, whose repertoire included a spectacular 'scorpion' kick, blundered by being caught in possession near the halfway line to concede the decisive goal as Colombia lost 2–1 to Cameroon in 1990?

11 Which record set by Fabian Barthez in 1998 was equalled by Gianluigi Buffon in 2006 and Iker Casillas in 2010?

17

Showmen

From a goldilocks perm to pioneering extravagant goal celebrations, the World Cup provides a platform for the finest showmen in the game to entertain. For the very best, the magicians with a wand in each boot, their sorcery brought the ultimate success. But even the bit-part performers have left their mark on tournaments with moments of sheer brilliance.

1 Pelé won the World Cup three times but was only voted as the best player in 1970. Which team-mates beat him to the Golden Ball award in 1958 and 1962?

2 Which trick, perfected to leave defenders flat-footed, was unveiled by the star of the 1974 World Cup – the only tournament in which he played – and still bears his name today?

3 Which of Diego Maradona's World Cup strikes was voted 'Goal of the Century' in a FIFA website poll in 2002?

4 Which Mexican striker celebrated his goals with a spectacular somersault, only seen once at the World Cup finals, after he netted against Belgium in the 1986 group stage?

5 Injury to which all-time great is seen by many as the key to Hungary's failure to lift the 1954 World Cup as he sat out two games and, after scoring the opening goal in the final, could not maintain his magic?

6 Who scored twice as a substitute in the 1970 tournament when a coach who could not choose between this Italian golden boy and the similarly talented Sandro Mazzola pursued a policy of switching the two at half-time?

7 Which mercurial player was described as 'daft as a brush' by his England manager Bobby Robson?

8 Which stylish midfielder, who guided his Romania side to the quarter-finals of the 1994 World Cup, was known as 'the Maradona of the Carpathians'?

9 What was the trademark goal celebration of Roger Milla, the Cameroon striker and oldest player to score in the finals with his strike against Russia in 1994?

10 Which temperamental genius finished joint top scorer at the 1994 World Cup with six goals, including the opener as Bulgaria stunned Germany in the quarter-finals?

11 Which Colombian midfielder known for his flamboyant hair styles shares his name with the venue for the 1997 Ryder Cup?

Bad Boys

Records indicate a certain confusion over the identity of the first player to be sent off at the finals and over the demands on match officials generally during the early years of the tournament, but there is no doubt referees in the modern day are rather busier than their predecessors. Almost as remarkable as the clouds of red and yellow cards hovering over every tournament are the reasons behind them, often when the stakes couldn't be higher.

1 Which Ghana striker, who later played in the English Premier League, missed the penalty awarded when Luis Suarez punched the ball away from Uruguay's goal line in a 2010 World Cup quarter-final?

2 Which Argentine player was given a police escort from the pitch when he initially refused to leave after being sent off in the 1966 World Cup quarter-final against England?

3 Which two players were sent off amid a high-profile spitting incident during the match between West Germany and the Netherlands at the 1990 World Cup?

4 Which record set by Rigobert Song in 1998 was equalled by Zinedine Zidane in 2006?

5 Which player infuriated England fans by winking to players and officials on his team's bench after Wayne Rooney was sent off at the 2006 World Cup?

6 Which player, famed for the magical ability that helped his side win the World Cup, exited in disgrace after failing a drug test at the 1994 World Cup?

7 Uruguay's José Batista recorded the fastest sending off in a match at the finals when he was dismissed 56 seconds into his team's 1986 group game against Scotland, for a foul on which opponent?

8 Referee Howard Webb brandished 14 yellow cards during the 2010 final but only sent off one player. Which one?

9 Which nation pulled off one of the biggest shocks in World Cup history in 1990, beating the holders after having two men sent off?

10 Why was England's Ray Wilkins sent off during a group game against Morocco at the 1986 World Cup?

11 Which team was the first to have a player sent off in a World Cup final and then had a second dismissed in the same match?

Memory Matches

While recognising that football will occasionally throw up a scintillating 0–0 draw, the most memorable encounters usually combine goals with the big occasion presented by a clash between two teams at the top of the game or by a minnow pushing a so-called superpower to the limit.

1 Which player scored four goals for Brazil as they opened their 1938 campaign with a 6–5 win over debut boys Poland and progressed to the semi-finals, where they rested the man who would become the tournament's top scorer – and lost to Italy!

2 The Scottish referee may have lived up to his name – Charlie Faultless – during the 1954 tournament quarter-finals, so what did Switzerland blame as they let slip a 3–0 lead over Austria to lose by a record-breaking 7–5?

3 Brazil's 5–2 win over Sweden in 1958 was the highest score in a World Cup final. Who were the only opponents to avoid defeat as they progressed to their first title?

4 North Korea were eliminated from the 1966 World Cup at the quarter-final stage after a memorable 5–3 defeat against Portugal. Who did they meet in their next match at the finals?

5 When Gordon Banks was taken ill prior to England's 1970 quarter-final against West Germany, which goalkeeper replaced him for the 3–2 defeat?

6   Sándor Kocsis of Hungary became the first player to do
    what in the finals, as his team beat South Korea 9–0 and
    West Germany 8–3 in 1954?

7   Which player struck twice from the penalty spot as
    England came from behind in 1990 to deny Cameroon
    the distinction of becoming the first African team to
    reach the semi-finals?

8   Which player stunned 1982 tournament favourites Brazil
    with a hat-trick as Italy came from behind to complete a
    remarkable 3–2 win?

9   Uruguay had never lost a World Cup match when they
    arrived in Lausanne for their semi-final in 1954, but
    which team beat them 4–2 in a contest considered to
    be one of the best in the history of the tournament?

10 The biggest crowd in World Cup finals history – nearly
    178,000 according to FIFA's data – squeezed into the
    Maracana to see the decisive game in the final group
    in 1950. Who were the teams and what was the score?

11 A pulsating play-off for third place in 2010 brought a
    3–2 win for Germany and extended Uruguay's failure
    to overcome European opposition at the World Cup.
    Who was the last European nation they beat, back in 1970?

Round 20

Biggest Wins

Often the sign of a mismatch, but not always. The tournament strategy which places huge importance on avoiding defeat in the first match also relies on rattling in the goals against the underdogs of the group. But sometimes, as demonstrated by Uruguay's 1986 experience, a meeting of equals can become a rout.

1 Hosts and eventual winners Italy scored more goals in their opening match in 1934 than they did in all of the remaining four games. Who did they beat 7–1?

2 Failure to qualify for the World Cup since their only tournament in 1938 has left Cuba with a long wait to avenge an 8–0 defeat against which seasoned European campaigners?

3 Portugal managed a meagre two shots on goal in their opening match against Ivory Coast in 2010 before the floodgates opened with a 7–0 win over which old rivals from 44 years earlier?

4 Which nation has qualified for the finals on every occasion since 2002, when they missed out despite rattling in 31 goals without reply against American Samoa?

5 Haiti actually took the lead in their first match at the World Cup finals before losing 3–1 to Italy and then being hammered 7–0 against which surprise package of the 1974 tournament?

6 Which team thrashed Zaire 9–0 in 1974 to ensure they progressed from Scotland's group on goal difference?

7 Hungary failed to reach the knockout stages in the 1982 tournament despite handing a record 10–1 beating to which opponents?

8 Only the vagaries of the tournament format kept Uruguay in the competition after they crashed 6–1 in 1986 to which team who were then dumped out of the knockout stage 5–1 by Spain?

9 If Saudi Arabia's highlight during four consecutive tournaments was reaching the knockout stages in 1994 the low was undoubtedly the 8–0 defeat in 2002 which featured a hat-trick by which German striker?

10 Which South American team, who contested the first World Cup but had to wait until their third tournament in 1994 for their first goal, came unstuck in spectacular fashion in 1950, losing 8–0 to continental cousins Uruguay?

11 Which Home Nation suffered the heaviest defeat in their history at the 1954 World Cup, losing 7–0 to Uruguay in the group stage?

Gaffers

One feature as the World Cup has progressed has been the emergence of heroes who competed as players and returned in later years as coaches, sometimes achieving double success. Another is the nomadic nature of coaches leading nations other than their own to the finals, although there are earlier examples.

1　George Raynor, whose career included spells in charge of Lazio, Coventry City and Doncaster Rovers, managed which nation at the 1950 and 1958 finals?

2　Which famous touchline chain-smoker led Argentina to two World Cup finals, winning the trophy in 1978?

3　Who was the first man to win the World Cup as captain of his team and then as coach?

4   Which manager led England to their first four World Cup finals and was replaced with Alf Ramsey after the 1962 tournament?

5   Which manager took Brazil to the World Cup finals in 2002 and repeated the achievement with Portugal in 2006?

6   Which controversial figure represented his country at four World Cup finals as a player – winning the trophy once – and returned in 2010 as coach?

7   What was the name given to the playing style developed by the Netherlands under coach Rinus Michels during the 1970s?

8   Which nation did former England boss Sven-Göran Eriksson manage during the 2010 World Cup finals?

9   What was achieved by Vittorio Pozzo at the 1938 World Cup in France?

10 Who captained Brazil to World Cup glory in 1994 but could only reach the quarter-finals as coach of the team at the 2010 tournament?

11 Which manager took Switzerland to the last 16 of the World Cup in 1994, their first appearance in the finals since 1966?

Round 22

Group of Death

Every World Cup has one, and this is our equivalent.
On the face of it, 11 tough questions with no margin for
error. But rather like Serbia and Montenegro in 2002 or the
United States in 2006, some of them might just be punching
above their weight.

1   Which two sides met in the quarter-finals in 1962 for
    the third consecutive tournament?

2   Of the 352 players selected for the squads in 1966, only
    eight played for teams outside their own domestic
    leagues. Which three nations did they represent in the
    finals?

3   What was Silvio Gazzaniga's contribution to World Cup
    football in 1974?

4 A qualifying tournament was introduced for the 1934 tournament and attracted 27 teams. For 2010 the total was 200. For which tournament did the number exceed 100 for the first time?

5 What was introduced by FIFA for the 1994 tournament and awarded to Brazil, France (1998), South Korea (2002) and Portugal (2006) but not given at all in 2010?

6 Who, in 1974, was elected as FIFA's first President from outside Europe after promising to increase the number of teams in the finals and create more opportunities for Africa and Asia?

7 England qualified for the 1982 finals despite the best efforts of which team, prompting commentator Bjørge Lillelien to declare, 'Your boys took a hell of a beating!'

8 One player scored both hat-tricks at the 1970 finals. Who was he?

9 Which player scored Scotland's only goal at the 1986 finals?

10 Which team was the first in World Cup history to beat Brazil by a three-goal margin?

11 Former England goalkeeper and Plymouth Argyle manager Tony Waiters led which team to the 1986 World Cup finals?

Round

23

Firsts

During the 19 tournaments which comprised the first 80 years of the World Cup the totals trumpeted by the organisers included 2,208 goals scored by 76 teams in 772 games, watched by just over 34 million spectators. Germany played the most matches, making them the first team to reach 100 with their opener in 2014 against Portugal. Here are a few more 'firsts'.

1   Which player scored the first hat-trick in a World Cup final?

2   What was first worn at the finals by players during the 1938 tournament in France?

3   Mexico's Juan Basaguren became the first substitute to do what in the World Cup finals when he played against El Salvador in the tournament in his home country in 1970?

4 Which World Cup first was recorded during the semi-final between West Germany and France in Spain in 1982?

5 During the 2006 tournament in Germany, which team became the first to be eliminated from the World Cup finals without conceding a goal?

6 Who were the first team to fail to score in a World Cup final?

7 Which team won the first-ever World Cup match, beating Mexico 4–1 in the Pocitos suburb of Montevideo on 13 July 1930 in front of a crowd of around 1,000?

8 At which World Cup was drug testing used for the first time?

9 Robert Prosinecki became the first player to score for two different countries at the World Cup finals. He netted for Yugoslavia in 1990 and for which team eight years later?

10 Which nation in 1934 was the first from Africa to enter the World Cup?

11 What was needed for the first time in the World Cup finals when Austria played France in 1938?

Club Connections

A round which gives an idea of the impact of international football on our domestic game. The players listed in each question below have all played for their country at the World Cup finals and for the same club in England, albeit maybe at different times and possibly on loan. Name their English clubs.

1. Jan Åge Fjørtoft (Norway),
   Jaime Moreno (Bolivia),
   Robert Huth (Germany).

2. Jimmy Floyd Hasselbaink (Netherlands),
   Junichi Inamoto (Japan),
   Gary Medel (Chile).

3 Ulises de la Cruz (Ecuador),
   Radhi Jaïdi (Tunisia),
   Christophe Dugarry (France).

4 Geremi (Cameroon),
   Jon Dahl Tomasson (Denmark),
   Stéphane Guivarc'h (France).

5 Wim Jonk (Netherlands),
   Dan Petrescu (Romania),
   John Harkes (United States)

6 Håkan Mild (Sweden),
   Øyvind Leonhardsen (Norway),
   Robbie Earle (Jamaica).

7 Richard Garcia (Australia),
   Robert Koren (Slovenia),
   Theodore Whitmore (Jamaica).

8 Thomas Gravesen (Denmark),
   Slaven Bilić (Croatia),
   Steven Pienaar (South Africa).

9   Fitzroy Simpson (Jamaica),
    Nwankwo Kanu (Nigeria),
    Niko Kranjčar (Croatia).

10 Lars Bohinen (Norway),
    Bryan Roy (Netherlands),
    Stern John (Trinidad and Tobago).

11 Fernando Hierro (Spain),
    Youri Djorkaeff (France),
    Hidetoshi Nakata (Japan).

Import Invasion

When the Premier League kicked off in 1992 the squads on the opening day featured just 16 players from outside the UK and Ireland. How much do you remember about some of the players who moved to England before and after that date having impressed on the biggest stage of all?

1 Dennis Bergkamp was one of Arsenal's most successful overseas signings, arriving in North London a year after scoring three goals at the 1994 World Cup. Which manager signed him?

2 Jay-Jay Okocha joined Bolton Wanderers after his third World Cup with Nigeria in 2002, but which English club did he help to promotion to the Premier League before retiring in 2008?

3 Which club moved to bring Carlos Tevez to the Premier
   League after his eye-catching performances for
   Argentina at the 2006 World Cup finals?

4 Dietmar Hamann was on the books of which Premier
   League club when he scored the last goal at the old
   Wembley Stadium, as Germany beat England in a
   qualifier for the 2002 World Cup?

5 Which striker was signed by Tottenham Hotspur after
   scoring three goals for the Belgium side that finished
   fourth at the 1986 World Cup?

6 A star of the Poland side at the 1974 and 1978
   World Cups, which English club did Kazimierz Deyna
   join after the tournament in Argentina?

7 Which controversial figure played for clubs including
   Sunderland, Blackburn Rovers and Doncaster Rovers
   after initially being signed by Liverpool following an
   impressive 2002 World Cup with Senegal?

8 Which player was signed by Blackburn Rovers a year after starring for Paraguay at the 2006 World Cup, proving a success during two years at Ewood Park and then moving to Manchester City where the goals dried up?

9 Which member of Brazil's 2002 World Cup-winning team joined Manchester United the following year but made just 20 Premier League appearances in two injury-hit seasons before departing for Beşiktaş?

10 Which Chelsea legend played just one match at the finals, coming on as substitute for Italy against Nigeria in 1994 and collecting two yellow cards, departing after just 12 minutes on the pitch?

11 One who went the other way was David Platt, who alerted continental clubs with his energy and a stunning, last-gasp goal for England against Belgium at the 1990 World Cup. For which Italian club did he leave Aston Villa?

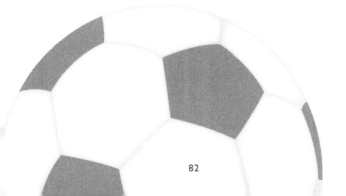

One-Offs

Bosnia and Herzegovina was the only first-time qualifier for the 2014 World Cup finals, taking the total number of teams to have competed only once to 15. Some, such as Senegal and Ukraine, can be expected to return, but not East Germany or Dutch East Indies. Some have made more impact than others, although not always for the right reasons.

1   Which nation made its only World Cup finals appearances in 1998 and bounced back from defeats against Croatia and Argentina to beat emerging force Japan 2–1 in their last match?

2   Which nation's main contribution to World Cup history was political – the team no one wanted to play – until they performed at the finals for the only time in 1970?

3 Which coach, who later led Brazil to World Cup glory in 1994, managed Kuwait for their only finals campaign in 1982?

4 How did Ernst Jean-Joseph hit the headlines as a member of the Haiti team which competed in the World Cup finals for the only time in 1974?

5 Thierry Henry came up against which Arsenal team-mate as France inflicted a third tournament defeat on Togo who were playing in their only finals in 2006?

6 Senegal reached the finals for the only time in 2002 and stunned a succession of more established teams before falling to which nation in the quarter-finals?

7 Who finished as top scorer for Bosnia and Herzegovina during the qualifying campaign which took them to the 2014 finals, their first since gaining independence from Yugoslavia?

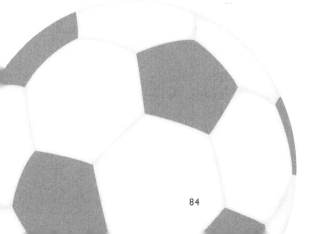

8   Which giant of global politics and culture played at the
    World Cup finals for the only time in 2002 and made
    the short journey home with no points and no goals?

9   The format of the 1938 finals was such that the Dutch
    East Indies travelled all the way to France to play just
    one match in their only tournament, losing 6–0 to
    which powerhouse of European football?

10 Which Premier League goalkeeper kept out the likes
    of Freddie Ljungberg, Henrik Larsson and Zlatan
    Ibrahimović as Trinidad and Tobago secured their only
    point in their only finals with a goalless draw against
    Sweden in 2006?

11 Ukraine reached the quarter-finals of the 2006
    World Cup but were denied the chance of a second
    tournament by defeat against which nation in the
    play-offs for the 2014 competition?

Round

27

Absent Friends

Perhaps the greatest sadness of the World Cup is that so many truly great players miss out on the tournament because their country didn't qualify at the right time, or in some cases at all. In tennis or golf a world-class performer can make their mark in a Grand Slam or a Major. In cricket and both codes of rugby, the finals can easily accommodate the major nations and top players, if available. But some of the players who have missed out in football would be candidates for a World XI.

1 Which Manchester United legend made 37 starts for Northern Ireland between 1964 and 1977 but was not selected when his country qualified for the World Cup finals in 1982?

2 Which player scored the only goal as Ireland beat Brazil in a friendly in 1987 but had retired from the international game by the time Jack Charlton picked his squad for Italia 90?

3 George Weah was voted World Player of the Year in 1995 but as a Liberia international never made it to the World Cup. Which English Premier League club did he join on loan from Milan in 2000?

4 Which Manchester United star, who won every honour in the game with his club, is one of many great Wales players never to have appeared in the World Cup finals?

5 Which two Old Firm rivals served with distinction as captains of Scotland and as captains and managers of their clubs during the 1960s and early 1970s but never reached the World Cup finals?

6 Didier Deschamps lifted the World Cup for France but was described as a 'water carrier' by which legendary player who never appeared in the finals?

7 Which lively forward, whose clubs included Ajax, Barcelona and Liverpool, never made it to the World Cup finals because he played for Finland?

8   Which classy midfielder shone for Barcelona and Real Madrid and won the 1980 European Championships with West Germany but was not selected for the 1982 World Cup finals and retired from international football in 1984 at the age of 24?

9   Which player was selected by Sir Alf Ramsey for the 1970 World Cup squad but never played a match and then captained club and country as England failed to qualify during the rest of the decade?

10 Which player, who turned out for four clubs in the English Premier League, never featured in the World Cup finals for France after being blamed for their qualifying defeat against Bulgaria in 1993?

11 Who played international football for Argentina, Colombia and Spain and won five consecutive European Cups with Real Madrid but never appeared at the World Cup finals?

TV Teams

Publican and postman were two jobs that suited players once they hung up their boots, but increasingly pundit can be added to the list. And just as the on-field action has gained a greater international influence the analysis in the studio has followed suit. During any World Cup the BBC and ITV can be expected to unveil an array of experts, some of them from the pinnacle of the world game.

1   Which TV pundit played in all three of Scotland's games at the 1982 World Cup finals but was not selected for the squad four years later?

2   Which former chairman of the Professional Footballers' Association never played international football but joined ITV's punditry team for 2014 after impressing on *Countdown* and *Question Time*?

3   Which former England full-back impressed viewers as
    a pundit for BBC TV but switched channels to ITV
    during 2012?

4   Which player, whose clubs included Brighton and
    Liverpool, retired too early to contribute to Ireland's
    World Cup campaigns but later made his mark with the
    Spanish media and covered the 1990 finals?

5   Which former England player whose TV roles
    included a pizza advert poking fun at his missed penalty
    gave up a punditry role with ITV to work with the
    Football Association?

6   Injury hampered the international careers of occasional
    pundits Trevor Brooking and Kevin Keegan.
    Against which opponents did they both come on as
    substitutes in 1982 to make their only World Cup
    finals appearances?

7   Which player who made three appearances for Italy
    at the 1990 World Cup combined media work at
    Sky Sports and the BBC with playing and management
    roles at Chelsea and Watford?

8   BBC TV sports presenter Gary Lineker spared England's
    blushes at the 1986 World Cup with a hat-trick against
    which opponents in the group matches?

9   Which Dutchman, who captained his nation at the 1990
    World Cup, became a regular pundit on British TV
    after moving into management with Chelsea and
    Newcastle United?

10 A World Cup winner with France in 1998, which former
    player joined the BBC's media team for the 2006
    World Cup two years after leaving Chelsea?

11 Which former player who earned more than 100 caps
    for Ireland – including all four matches at the
    2002 World Cup – has moved into the media with the
    BBC?

Name Game

Apologies in advance for this crackpot round of word play and excruciating puns. If you can make sense of the clues and come up with the answers you could be halfway to a job with a World Cup planning committee.

1   History shows us you can't have a World Cup without this Scotland striker from 1982.

2   You can make do with a lot of equipment in football but this England midfielder from 1966 is the most basic requirement.

3   For somewhere to play look no further than this coach
    who led the United States to the quarter-finals in 2002
    and secured qualification again in 2006.

4   Commercial success is ever important these days, so you
    need a quality Dutch midfielder from the 1970s to
    sign up some business sponsors and he can start with
    England's keeper from 1966 and 1970.

5   Thankfully the game is still all about the supporters,
    generating an excitement and atmosphere of their own,
    just like this legend of German World Cup history.

6   Football food is a challenge in the absence of players called
    'Pie'. Harry Haddock didn't get a game for Scotland
    in 1958 and Patrick Berger never made it to the finals
    so just tinker with the names of an England full-back
    and Irish defender, both from the 1990s, and a famous
    Costa Rica striker.

7   For transport you can call on two Japanese midfielders or an Irish full-back who missed the 2002 finals through injury. A more leisurely option might be a Scotland midfielder from 1982.

8   To reach the modern global audience you need saturation media coverage from a Brazil manager of the 1980s and the referee from the 2010 final.

9   Be sure to make plans for new and old media to capture the action with this hero of Senegal's 2002 World Cup campaign.

10 Essential preparations for armchair fans include a visit to this German striker from 2002, whether picking up a Swedish midfielder from 1994 or his nation's manager in 2002 and 2006.

11 With a nod to the creative forces behind Fantasy Football League all those years ago, to tidy up afterwards just whistle up this referee from the 2002 World Cup final.

Penalties

So here we are. The penalties at the end. Do it properly. Get everyone else to stand at the halfway line – the other end of the bar will suffice – and link arms while simultaneously trying to cover their eyes. Then find a bunch of people to hurl abuse at you while you think about a. how to answer the question and b. whose shirt you want to swap to wipe away those tears of joy or despair.

1   Which pop superstar made a comical hash of a penalty attempt during the opening ceremony of the 1994 World Cup?

2   And which football superstar hoisted the last penalty of that tournament high over the bar as Brazil beat Italy in the first shoot-out to settle a World Cup final?

3   Which player scored four times from the spot on his way to finishing the 1966 World Cup as top scorer with nine goals?

4   No penalties had been awarded in the World Cup
    final prior to 1974 and then two came along at once!
    Which players scored them?

5   Which player scored from the spot to give his team the
    lead in the 2006 World Cup final but couldn't help them
    in the penalty shoot-out as he had been sent off by then?

6   Which two legends of the game failed to convert their
    kicks as France beat Brazil in the shoot-out at the end
    of their 1986 World Cup quarter-final?

7   Which team in 2006 became the first to fail to score
    in a World Cup penalty shoot-out?

8   Argentina's first penalty shoot-out defeat at a
    World Cup came in the quarter-finals in 2006,
    but against which opponents?

9   Which team in 1998 became the first to lose three penalty
    shoot-outs in the World Cup finals?

10 Who was the first person to miss a penalty at the
    World Cup finals?

11 After FIFA introduced the 'golden goal' rule for the
    1998 World Cup finals, how many of the four matches
    that entered extra time proceeded to be settled
    by penalties?

THE ANSWERS

1 Ayresome Park, Middlesbrough.
2 Franz Beckenbauer.
3 Argentina.
4 Bulgaria.
5 A lion.
6 Pak Doo-Ik.
7 Eusebio, of Portugal.
8 Uruguay.
9 Portugal.
10 Portugal, beating Russia.
11 Kenneth Wolstenholme.

Round 2 **England**

1 Bobby Charlton.
2 Scotland.
3 Fabio Capello.
4 Stan Mortensen.
5 Bobby Robson.
6 Matthew Upson.
7 Owen Hargreaves.
8 Geoff Hurst.
9 Eileen Drewery.
10 A turnip.
11 The metatarsal bones.

Northern Ireland

1 Norman Whiteside.
2 Billy Bingham.
3 Because the tournament schedule demanded that matches be played on a Sunday.
4 David Healy.
5 Pat Jennings.
6 Peter McParland.
7 Gerry Armstrong.
8 France.
9 Colin Clarke.
10 Martin Paterson.
11 Harry Gregg.

Republic of Ireland

1 England.
2 David O'Leary.
3 All four teams finished with the same number of points – four.
4 Because of arguments over water breaks for players in the intense heat.
5 Dennis Bergkamp.
6 They were the only players to score against Germany during the tournament.
7 Mick McCarthy.
8 Iran.
9 Niall Quinn.
10 Thierry Henry.
11 Kevin Sheedy.

Round 5

Scotland

1 Archie Gemmill.
2 Australia.
3 Tommy Docherty and Willie Ormond.
4 Alex Ferguson.
5 Morocco.
6 They were forced to go through the motions of kicking off a World Cup qualifier even though hosts Estonia had not turned up due to a dispute over the start time.
7 The Soviet Union.
8 He resigned before the first match.
9 They were the first team in World Cup history to be eliminated without losing a match.
10 Berti Vogts.
11 Joe Jordan.

Round 6 — **Wales**

1 Chewing gum.
2 Ninian Park, Cardiff.
3 John Charles.
4 Pelé.
5 Scotland.
6 Anfield, Liverpool.
7 Ryan Giggs and Ian Rush.
8 San Marino.
9 Juventus.
10 Iceland.
11 Ivor Allchurch.

Brazil

1 Hungary.
2 England.
3 Goodison Park.
4 He scored in every match played by his team during the tournament.
5 Sweden.
6 Sócrates.
7 France.
8 Ronaldo.
9 Turkey.
10 Mário Zagallo.
11 Pelé.

Winners

1 As hosts four years earlier they felt they had been snubbed by European nations.
2 Italy, winning in France in 1938.
3 East Germany.
4 Defender Laurent Blanc kissing goalkeeper Fabien Barthez on the head.
5 David Villa.
6 Ipswich Town.
7 Valencia.
8 England's Michael Owen.
9 Brazil.
10 The World Cup final in 2002.
11 Pelé.

Round 9

Venues

1 It was the first World Cup fixture to be played indoors.
2 Qatar.
3 The vuvuzela.
4 At 2,665m above sea level, it was the highest altitude for a World Cup finals match.
5 Because Wembley had a prior engagement with a greyhound race meeting.
6 Colombia.
7 South Africa.
8 South Korea and Japan.
9 West Germany.
10 Montevideo.
11 West Germany, with six attempts.

Round 10

Upsets

1 He scored the goal that earned the United States victory over England in 1950.
2 Italy.
3 Ray Houghton.
4 New Zealand.
5 Saudi Arabia.
6 Tunisia.
7 François Omam-Biyik.
8 Morocco.
9 Iran.
10 Fulham.
11 Uruguay.

Round 11 Controversies

1 His own goal against the United States.
2 El Salvador and Honduras.
3 Roy Keane.
4 Patrick Battiston.
5 Russian (originally from Azerbaijan, then part of the Soviet Union).
6 Maniche.
7 Willie Johnston.
8 Algeria.
9 South Africa.
10 Vanessa Perroncel.
11 Marco Materazzi.

Round 12 Howlers

1 Pickles.
2 The corner flags.
3 Graham Poll.
4 While awaiting a free-kick he raced from his position in the defensive wall and hoofed the ball back up the pitch.
5 Ronaldinho.
6 Nicolas Anelka.
7 'Vindaloo'.
8 Gary Lineker.
9 Ronaldo.
10 Rivaldo.
11 The Netherlands.

No Easy Games?

1 Belgium.
2 Mexico.
3 Israel.
4 1974, in West Germany.
5 A leopard.
6 Cameroon.
7 A tie.
8 Jorge 'George' Robledo.
9 Uwe Seeler.
10 East Germany.
11 Tunisia.

Round 14 Open Goals

1 Uruguay.
2 South Africa.
3 Jules Rimet.
4 Don Revie.
5 Scotland.
6 Brazil.
7 1958.
8 *It's A Knockout.*
9 It was the official match ball of the tournament.
10 Alf Ramsey, for the 1974 finals.
11 Score a hat-trick.

Marksmen

1 Jimmy Greaves.
2 Jurgen Klinsmann.
3 Paolo Rossi.
4 Ronaldo.
5 Eusébio.
6 Grzegorz Lato.
7 Just Fontaine.
8 Davor Šuker.
9 Peru.
10 Oleg Salenko.
11 Gabriel Batistuta.

Keepers

1 Lev Yashin.
2 Michel Preud'homme of Belgium.
3 Pelé.
4 Jan Tomaszewski.
5 Dino Zoff.
6 Sergio Goycochea.
7 José Luis Chilavert.
8 Gilmar.
9 England.
10 René Higuita.
11 Only two goals conceded, the lowest number by a World Cup-winning side.

Showmen

1   Didi in 1958 and Garrincha in 1962.
2   The Cruyff Turn.
3   His second against England in 1986.
4   Hugo Sánchez.
5   Ferenc Puskás.
6   Gianni Rivera.
7   Paul Gascoigne.
8   Gheorghe Hagi.
9   He danced around the corner post.
10   Hristo Stoichkov.
11   Carlos Valderrama.

Round 18 — Bad Boys

1 Asamoah Gyan.
2 Antonio Rattin.
3 Rudi Völler of West Germany and Frank Rijkaard of the Netherlands.
4 Two red cards during the World Cup finals tournaments.
5 Cristiano Ronaldo.
6 Diego Maradona.
7 Gordon Strachan.
8 John Heitinga.
9 Cameroon.
10 For throwing the ball at the referee.
11 Argentina, against West Germany in 1990.

Memory Matches

1. Leônidas.
2. The glare of the sun.
3. England.
4. Brazil, in 2010.
5. Peter Bonetti.
6. Score two hat-tricks.
7. Gary Lineker.
8. Paolo Rossi.
9. Hungary.
10. Uruguay beat Brazil 2–1.
11. Russia.

Biggest Wins

1 The United States.
2 Sweden.
3 North Korea.
4 Australia.
5 Poland.
6 Yugoslavia.
7 El Salvador.
8 Denmark.
9 Miroslav Klose.
10 Bolivia.
11 Scotland.

1 Sweden.
2 César Luis Menotti.
3 Franz Beckenbauer.
4 Walter Winterbottom.
5 Luiz Felipe Scolari.
6 Diego Maradona.
7 Total Football.
8 Ivory Coast.
9 He was the first coach to win the World Cup twice.
10 Dunga.
11 Roy Hodgson.

Round 22

Group of Death

1 Yugoslavia and West Germany.
2 Three played for Spain, three for West Germany and two for France.
3 He designed the new trophy.
4 1982, in Spain.
5 The award for the most entertaining team.
6 João Havelange.
7 Norway.
8 Gerd Müller of West Germany, against Bulgaria and Peru.
9 Gordon Strachan.
10 France, in the 1998 final.
11 Canada.

Firsts

1 Geoff Hurst.
2 Numbered shirts.
3 Score a goal.
4 The first penalty shoot-out.
5 Switzerland.
6 Argentina, in 1990.
7 France.
8 1966, in England.
9 Croatia.
10 Egypt.
11 Extra time.

Club Connections

1. Middlesbrough.
2. Cardiff City.
3. Birmingham City.
4. Newcastle United.
5. Sheffield Wednesday.
6. Wimbledon FC.
7. Hull City.
8. Everton.
9. Portsmouth.
10. Nottingham Forest.
11. Bolton Wanderers.

Round 25 — Import Invasion

1 Bruce Rioch.
2 Hull City.
3 West Ham United.
4 Liverpool.
5 Nico Claesen.
6 Manchester City.
7 El Hadji Diouf.
8 Roque Santa Cruz.
9 Kléberson.
10 Gianfranco Zola.
11 Bari.

1 Jamaica.
2 Israel.
3 Carlos Alberto Parreira.
4 He became the first player to fail a drug test.
5 Emmanuel Adebayor.
6 Turkey.
7 Edin Džeko.
8 China.
9 Hungary.
10 Shaka Hislop.
11 France.

Absent Friends

1 George Best.
2 Liam Brady.
3 Chelsea.
4 Ryan Giggs.
5 John Greig and Billy McNeill.
6 Eric Cantona.
7 Jari Litmanen.
8 Bernd Schuster.
9 Emlyn Hughes.
10 David Ginola.
11 Alfredo Di Stéfano.

Round 28

TV Teams

1 Alan Hansen.
2 Clark Carlisle.
3 Lee Dixon.
4 Michael Robinson.
5 Gareth Southgate.
6 Spain.
7 Gianluca Vialli.
8 Poland.
9 Ruud Gullit.
10 Marcel Desailly.
11 Kevin Kilbane.

Round 29 — Name Game

1. Alan Brazil.
2. Alan Ball.
3. Bruce Arena.
4. Johnny Rep and Gordon Banks.
5. Fans Beckenbauer.
6. Tony Dorito, Phil Ke-Babb and Paulo Wanchope.
7. Junichi Inamoto, Keisuke Honda, Steven Carr and John Wark.
8. Telê Santana and Howard Webb.
9. Henri Camara.
10. Oliver Bierhoff, Håkan Mild and Lars Lagerbäck.
11. Pierluigi (the) Collina.